BUILDING BLOCKS OF COMPUTER SCIENCE

CODING LANGUAGES

Written by Echo Elise González

Illustrated by Graham Ross

a Scott Fetzer company
Chicago

World Book, Inc.
180 North LaSalle Street
Suite 900
Chicago, Illinois 60601
USA

For information about other World Book publications, visit our website at **www.worldbook.com** or call **1-800-WORLDBK (967-5325).**
For information about sales to schools and libraries, call 1-800-975-3250 (United States), or 1-800-837-5365 (Canada).

Library of Congress Cataloging-in-Publication Data for this volume has been applied for.

Building Blocks of Computer Science
ISBN: 978-0-7166-2883-5 (set, hc.)

Coding Languages
ISBN: 978-0-7166-3383-9

Also available as:
ISBN: 978-0-7166-2894-1 (e-book)

1st printing August 2020

STAFF

Executive Committee
President: Geoff Broderick
Vice President, Finance: Donald D. Keller
Vice President, Marketing: Jean Lin
Vice President, International Sales: Maksim Rutenberg
Vice President, Technology: Jason Dole
Director, Editorial: Tom Evans
Director, Human Resources: Bev Ecker

Editorial
Manager, New Content: Jeff De La Rosa
Writer: Echo Elise González
Proofreader: Nathalie Strassheim

Digital
Director, Digital Product Development: Erika Meller
Digital Product Manager: Jon Wills

Graphics and Design
Sr. Visual Communications Designer: Melanie Bender
Coordinator, Design Development and Production: Brenda B. Tropinski
Sr. Web Designer/Digital Media Developer: Matt Carrington

Acknowledgments:
Art by Graham Ross/The Bright Agency
Series reviewed by Peter Jang/Actualize Coding Bootcamp

TABLE OF CONTENTS

There is a glossary on page 30. Terms defined in the glossary are in type **that looks like this** on their first appearance.

WHAT IS A CODING LANGUAGE?

Howdy!
I'm Zero.

And I'm One.

Coding languages are also called *programming languages.* Computer programmers use coding languages to give instructions to computers.
The human brain processes information much differently than does a computer.
say your name
When programmers think of something they want a computer to do, they must figure out how to communicate the instructions in a way the computer can understand.
They must know how to translate a human idea into a command for the computer, using coding languages.
Hi, my name is Jamal.
10101110
Tasky is the name.

Coders use high-level languages to write computer programs.

```
#Leap Year Check
if year % 4=0 and
year % 100!=0:
print (year, is a
leap year")
```

Those programs are then converted into low-level languages—such as **assembly language** and **machine language**—for the computer to read.

10101010111001010101010001
00101010001010010101010001
10110110001010110101001010
11001010100101010101000010
10101001010101000101010101

Assembly language is a language designed for one specific kind of **processor,** an information-processing **computer chip** that controls a computer system.

1010 101010101001010100
001010011010101010001101

Programmers usually write code in high-level languages because low-level languages are difficult for humans to work with.

10100101011010
10100010101010
00010011010100
10110101000110

High-level languages use familiar words and symbols in a way similar to human language and mathematics.

This similarity makes high-level languages much easier to write in than in the long, complex strings of **binary digits** that make up machine languages.

After a program is written, it is translated from the high-level language into a low-level language.

MACHINE LANGUAGE

Like humans, computers need their instructions given in a language they can understand.

Tasky the Robot, like all computers, understands **machine language.**

Instead of letters and words, machine language is made up of **bits.**

A bit is the tiniest piece of **data** a computer can store.

It's just a little bit of information... the littlest bit!

A bit can either be represented by a 0 or a 1.
Reading a bit triggers a tiny **circuit** within the computer.

Think of this circuit as a light switch. It can only be switched either ON or OFF.
ON
OFF

When Tasky reads a 1 in machine language, a circuit switches ON. When Tasky reads a 0, a circuit switches OFF.
ON
CLICK
CLICK
OFF

There are many circuits that carry information to Tasky's **processors.**
The more circuits a computer has, the more bits it can receive and store.

Information can be encoded in different combinations of **bits.**

A computer's memory, calculations, and other processes are stored and performed using the electrical signals carried by bits.
SIGNALS

Bits can be combined to represent a variety of information, such as letters, numbers, colors, and sounds.

The more bits that are combined, the more complex the meaning can be.

If we have two bits, there are only four possible combinations: 00, 01, 10, and 11. So we can represent four different things.

00, 01,
10, 11

01
00
11
10
For example, we could represent four different colors.

If we have three bits, then there are eight possible combinations: 000, 001, 011, 111, 110, 100, 010, and 101. Now we can represent eight different colors.
A group of 8 bits is called a **byte.**

000
010
111
001
011
110
100
101

If we have 4 bits, then there are 16 possible combinations to represent 16 different things.

A byte, 8 bits, can represent 256 different things.
A **gigabyte** is 1 billion bytes.

BING
ZOOM
Imagine how many different colors, sounds, commands, and other pieces of information can be represented in a 30-gigabyte video game!

HIGH-LEVEL LANGUAGES
Low-level languages can be very specific to one particular type of machine or even a single machine.
But **high-level languages** can be used on a variety of machines.
So, a programmer can use a high-level language to write a program that works on multiple different machines, not just one.

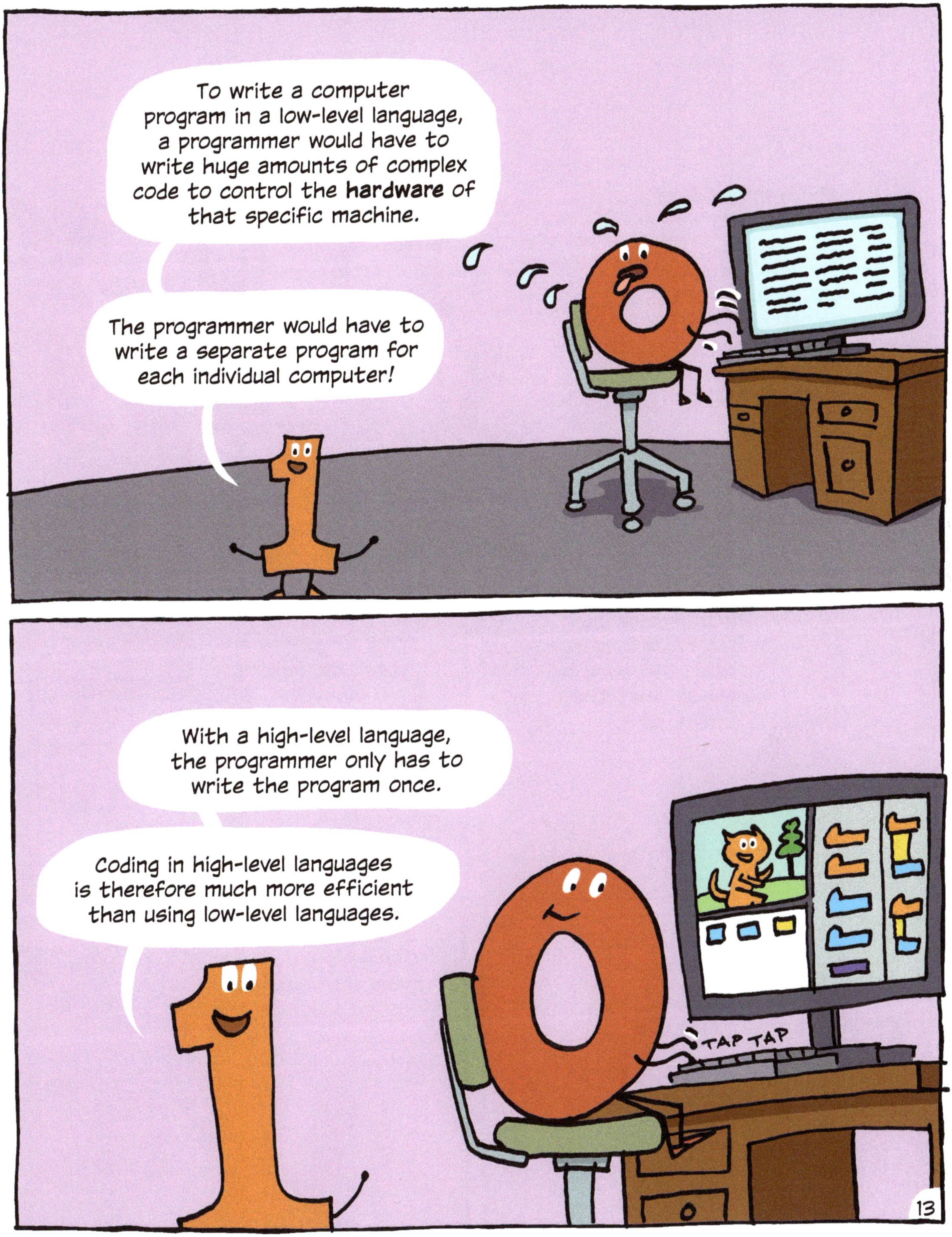

To write a computer program in a low-level language, a programmer would have to write huge amounts of complex code to control the **hardware** of that specific machine.

The programmer would have to write a separate program for each individual computer!

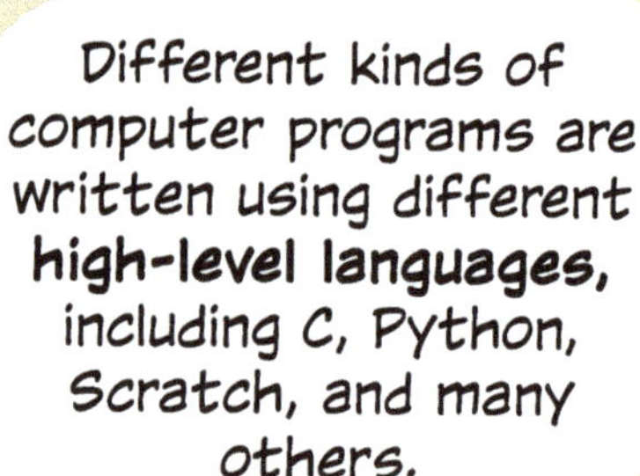
Different kinds of computer programs are written using different **high-level languages,** including C, Python, Scratch, and many others.

C
PYTHON
SCRATCH

Programmers can choose which language to learn and work in based on what they want to do.

Some languages are great for building websites.
WWW

Some can be used to make apps.

Others are used to make video games...
...or program robots.
Hi

Some languages are designed for a variety of uses. Others are designed for a specific purpose.
C
How are these languages different from one another?
PYTHON
To start, they use different sets of words and symbols.
They are also structured differently. The rules for structuring a line of **code** are different in each language.
SCRATCH

C
C language is a very useful **coding language.**
It is closer to **machine language** than are most other **high-level languages.**
This closeness to machine language gives the programmer a high degree of control over the program. It also enables the program to easily access a computer's memory and other **hardware** functions.

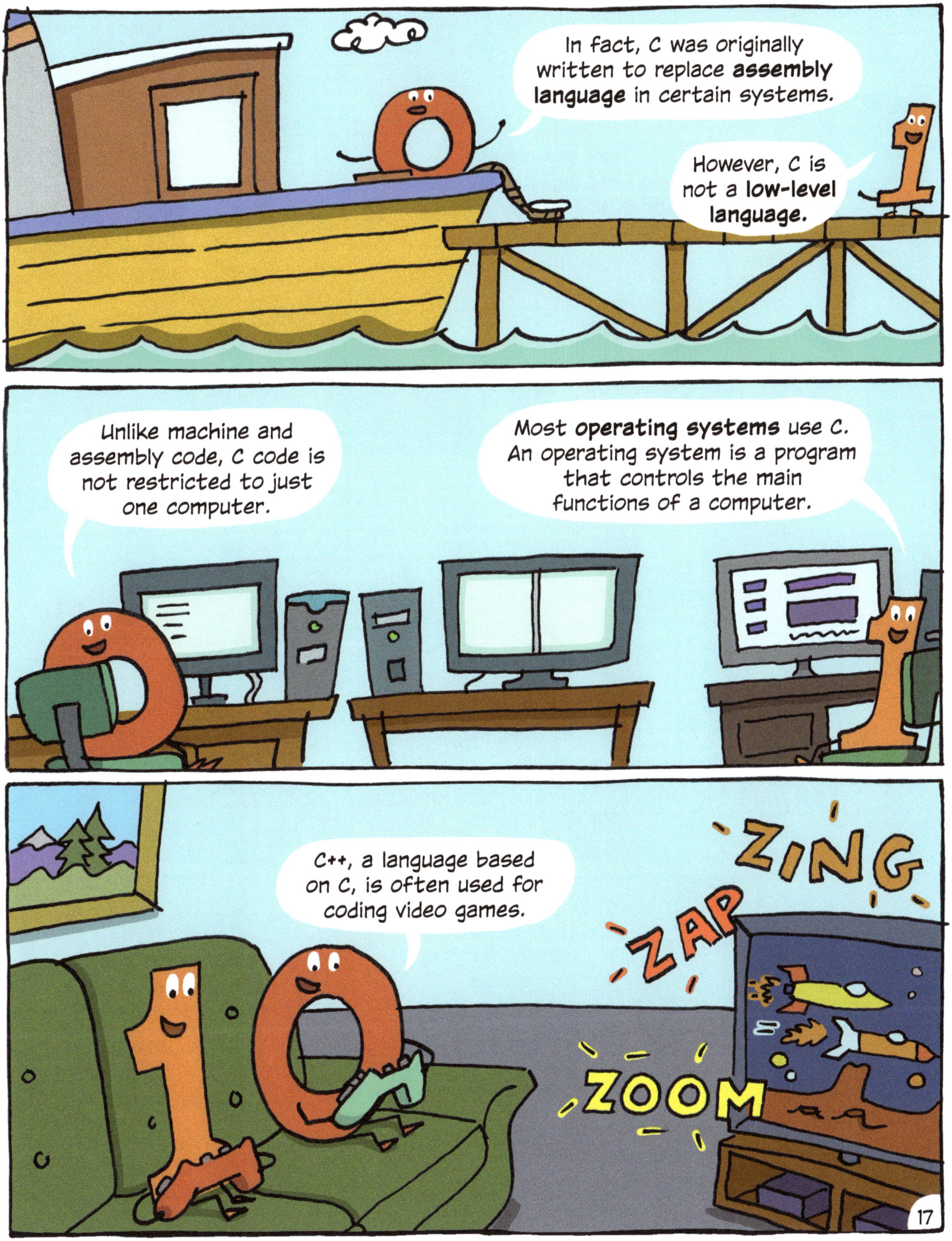

In fact, C was originally written to replace **assembly language** in certain systems.

However, C is not a **low-level language.**

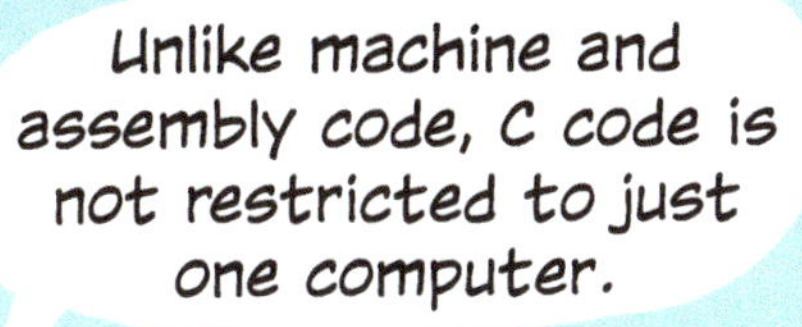

PYTHON
There are many **coding languages** that have their roots in C language.
One of the most popular is called Python.
But it wasn't named for the snake.
It was named after a British television comedy, *Monty Python's Flying Circus!*
Monty Python's
FLYING
CIRCUS

Python:

```
print("Hello World")
```

C++

```
//Hello World in C++ (pre-ISO)
#include <iostream.h>
main()
{
  cout<<"Hello World!"<<endl;
  return 0;
}
```

Java

```
//Hello World in Java
class HelloWorld{
  static public void main(String args[]){
    System.out printing("Hello World!");
  }
}
```

SCRATCH
Scratch is a **block-based language.**
Block-based languages are often used to teach programming basics to kids and beginners.
move 10 steps
say Hello for 2 seconds
turn 15 degrees
BLOCK BASED
<divclass="slide-blink text"><div>
<divclass="slide-cat-slide-1cat-1">div>
<divclass="slide-cat-slide-2cat-2"><div>
<divclass-"slide-cat-slide-3-cat-3"><div>
<divclass-"slide-cat-slide-4cat-4"><div>
</div>
TEXT BASED
Block-based programs are put together using visual elements, rather than plain text.
In Scratch, instructions are represented by blocks that can fit together like a puzzle.

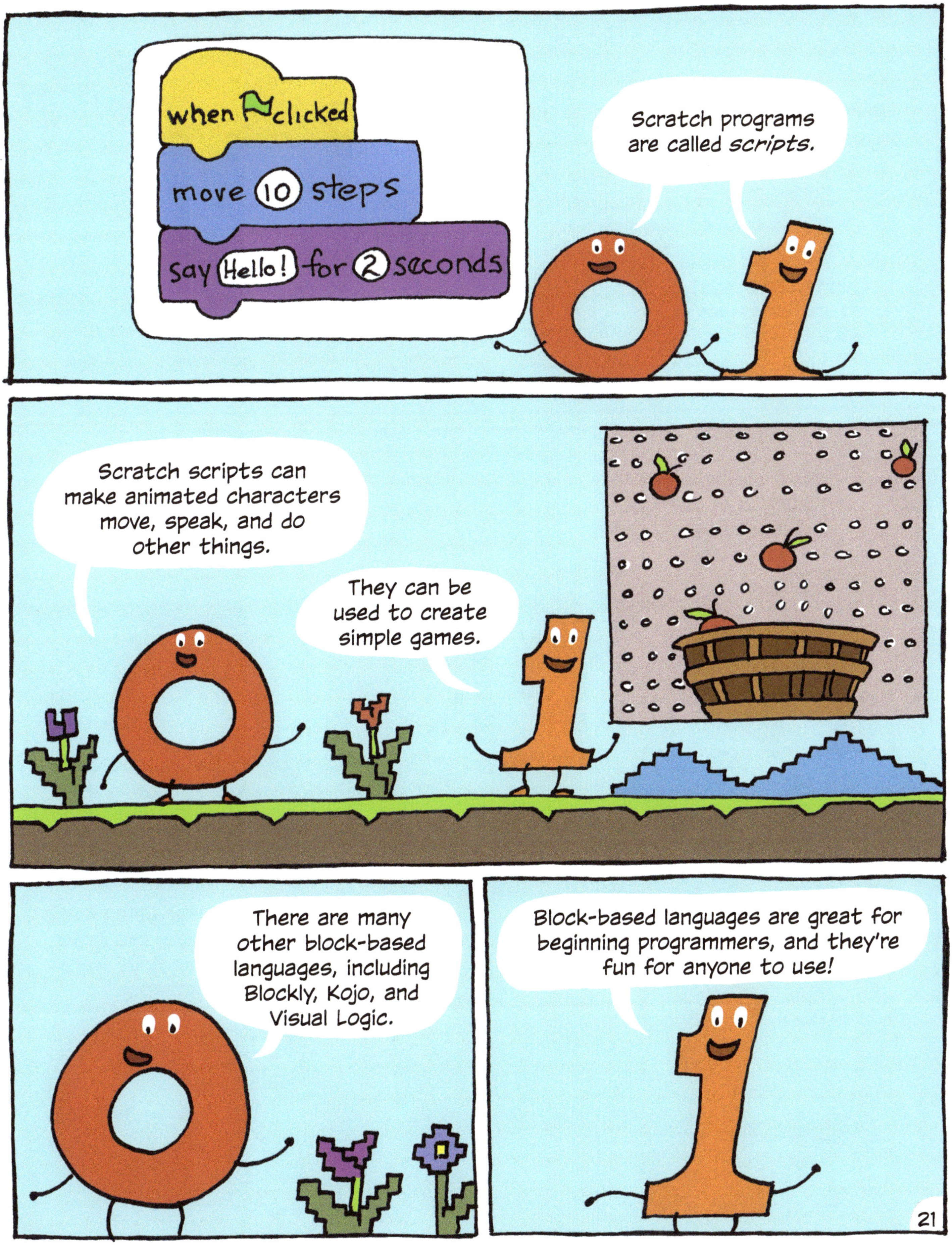

Scratch scripts can make animated characters move, speak, and do other things.

They can be used to create simple games.

SO, HOW DO THEY WORK?
Each **coding language** organizes and structures information in a unique way.
But there are some things that most coding languages have in common.
C++
Scratch
Python
Ruby
Perl
TAP TAP

Most coding languages make use of **syntax** to organize lines or blocks of **code.**
SYNTAX

The cat sat on the mat
Human languages also make use of syntax—the order and arrangement of words in a sentence.

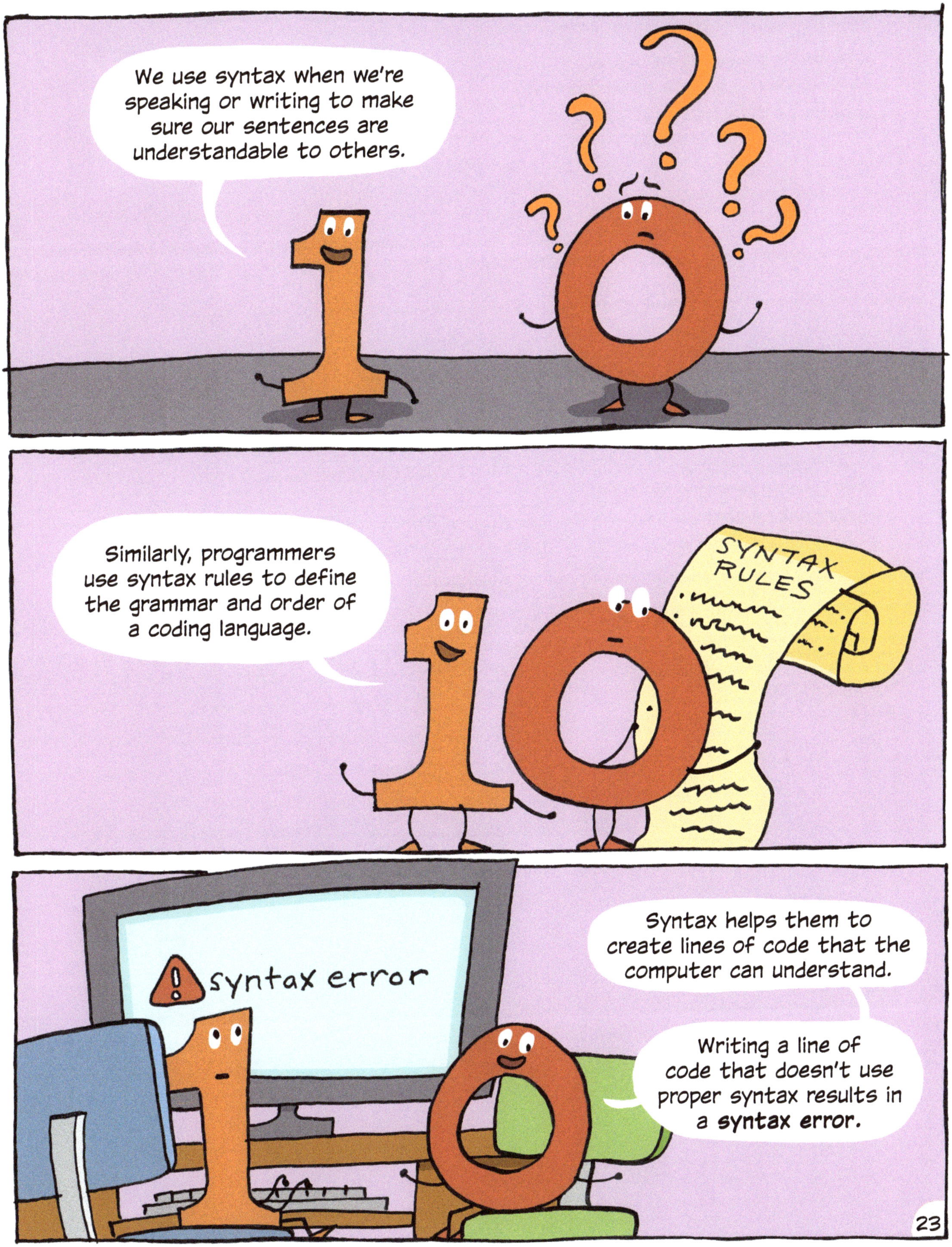

We use syntax when we're speaking or writing to make sure our sentences are understandable to others.

With a syntax in place, a programmer can use programming elements to write instructions for the computer.
tap
tap
Variables, loops, and conditions are all important elements of a coding language.
0
repeat 10
when space key pressed
Punctuation is also important.
Text-based programming languages use such punctuation as brackets, semicolons, and commas.
( )
{ }
;
,

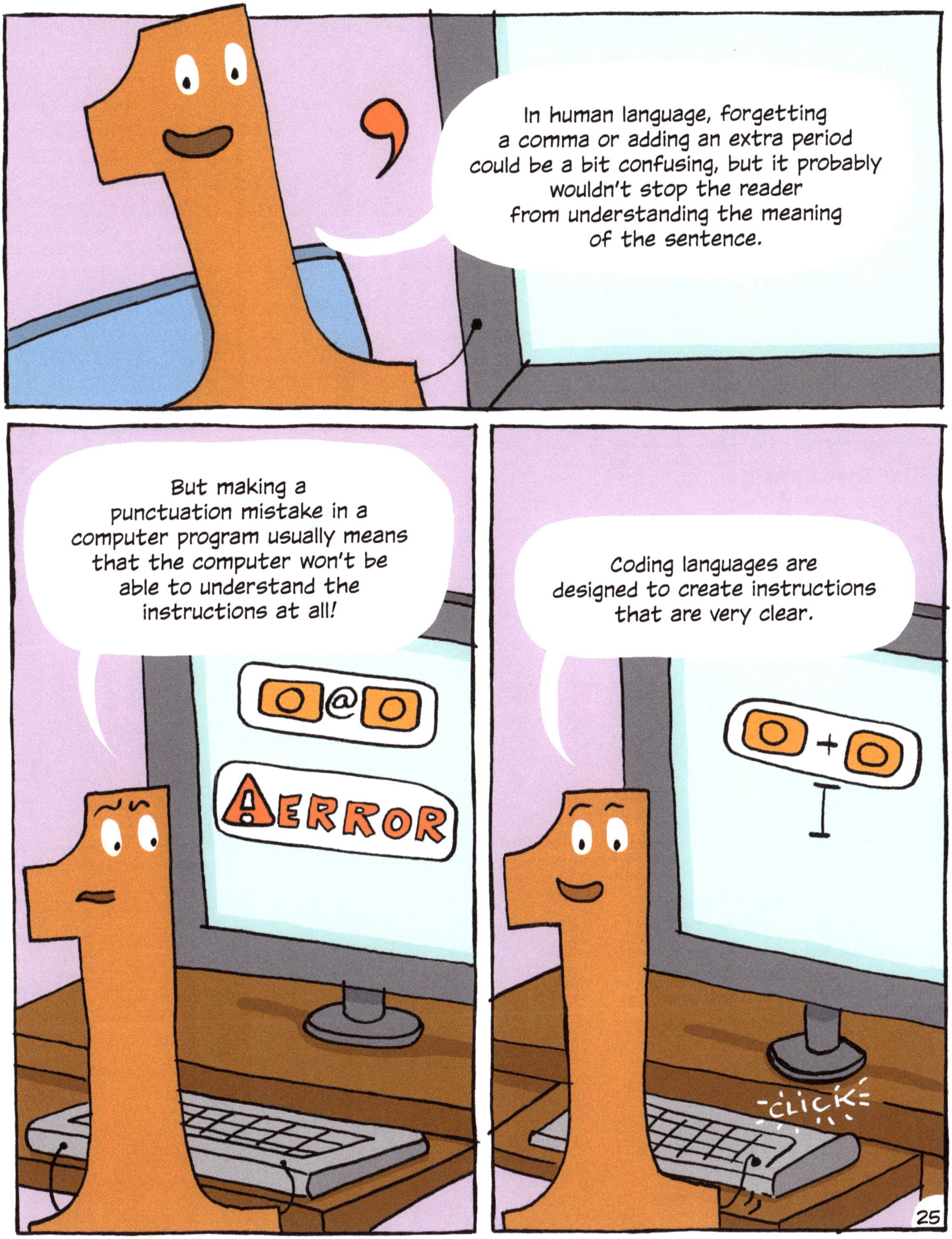

But making a punctuation mistake in a computer program usually means that the computer won't be able to understand the instructions at all!

@

ERROR

Coding languages are designed to create instructions that are very clear.

+

CLICK

TRANSLATING A PROGRAM

We used Python to write an app, and we want it to work on this phone.

I turn the assembly language into machine **code** that will send information to the phone's **circuits.**

ASSEMBLER

10100110101010

When the assembler has finished this part of the translation, the phone will be able to run our program!

Before compilers and assemblers were invented, programmers had to enter a ridiculous amount of 1's and 0's into a computer to program it.

This took a long time. It also made it very difficult to find programming errors.

WHICH CODING LANGUAGE SHOULD YOU LEARN?

We've talked about some of the most popular **coding languages.**

Now that you know how coding languages work, which ones would you like to learn?

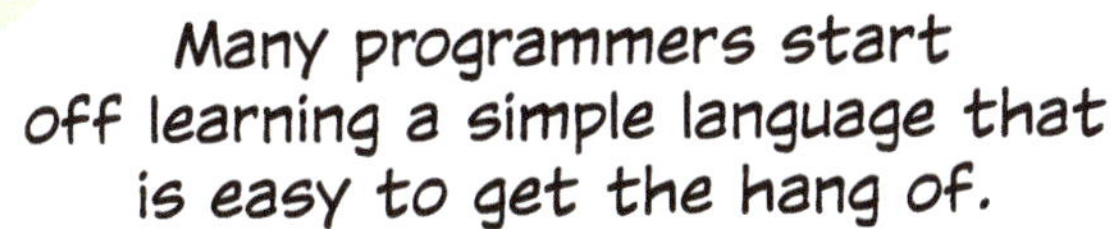
Many programmers start off learning a simple language that is easy to get the hang of.

Many want to learn a general-purpose language that can be used for as many applications as possible.

Others prefer to learn a language that is made for a specific purpose, such as developing **artificial intelligence** or working with **databases.**

Whichever language you end up learning, just remember: It's okay to take it slow.
If you're patient, you can learn as many as you like!
Maybe someday, you'll even create your own coding language!

GLOSSARY

artificial intelligence the ability of a computer system to process information in a manner similar to human thought or to exhibit humanlike behavior.

assembler a program that translates each command in an assembly language into a command in machine language.

assembly language a kind of low-level language. A program called an assembler translates assembly language into machine language.

binary digit a 0 or 1. These are the two digits that make up machine language.

bit the smallest piece of data a computer can store. A bit is represented by a 0 or a 1.

block-based language a programming language in which the programmer uses visual elements shaped like blocks to "build" a computer program.

byte a group of eight bits.

circuit a loop that an electric current can follow.

code instructions written in a programming language.

coding language (see programming language)

compiler a program that translates a high-level language into an assembly language.

computer chip a tiny piece of the material silicon that holds an electronic circuit.

condition a statement that can be true or false. A program may tell a computer to run a piece of code if a certain condition is true.

data information that a computer processes or stores.

database a collection of data organized so that a computer or a programmer can easily access the data.

gigabyte 1 billion bytes.

hardware the physical parts that make up computers and other electronics.

high-level language a programming language that uses symbols and words that human programmers can more easily understand. High-level languages are translated into low-level languages for the computer to understand.

loop a piece of code that causes part of a program to run over and over again.

low-level language the code used to communicate programs to a computer's hardware. High-level languages are translated into low-level languages for the computer to understand.

machine language the code used to communicate programs to a computer's hardware. Machine language is made up of binary digits.

operating system a program that controls the main functions of a computer.

processor a kind of computer chip that performs calculations for the computer.

programming language a set of symbols and rules that programmers use to write computer programs.

syntax the rules that make up the "grammar" of a programming language.

syntax error a computer error caused by improper syntax in the code.

variable a value, or piece of information, that can change.

GO ONLINE

Can you decode a secret message written in machine language? Go to this website to find the fun Binary Decoder activity!

www.worldbook.com/BuildingBlocks

You'll find all kinds of computer science activities and games to play.

INDEX

www.ingramcontent.com/pod-product-compliance
Ingram Content Group UK Ltd.
Pitfield, Milton Keynes, MK11 3LW, UK
UKHW061958290726
14090UKWH00021B/1266